How To Play
KEYBOARD

A Complete Guide
for Absolute Beginners

Ben Parker

Author: Ben Parker

Editor: Alison McNicol

First published in 2013 by Kyle Craig Publishing

This version updated Dec 2014

Text and illustration copyright © 2013 Kyle Craig Publishing

Design and illustration: Julie Anson

Music set by Ben Parker using Sibelius software

ISBN: 978-1-908707-14-7

A CIP record for this book is available from the British Library.

A Kyle Craig Publication
www.kyle-craig.com

Contents

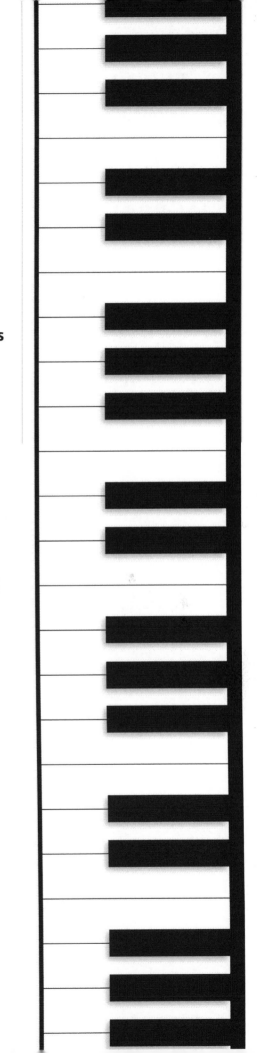

Introduction

Welcome to **How To Play Keyboard**. The electric keyboard is one of the most fun instruments to learn. With its range of sounds/tones and rhythms/beats, many beginners are playing their first tune within minutes. In this book we aim to give you your first simple steps to playing which can act as a basis for a bright future with any keyboard instrument. For those readers with no previous musical experience, also included in the book is a step by step guide to reading music.

 # Practice

Like any skill, playing an instrument takes a lot of practice. Practicing more regularly for shorter lengths of time is more effective than practicing for an hour or so just once a week. The minimum recommended amount would be around 15-20 minutes, 3 to 4 times a week. The ideal amount would be 20 minutes a day, 7 days a week. Perhaps set out a plan of your week and work out the best times to fit your practicing around the other things you do. The more your practice can become a part of your weekly or daily routine the better.

It is the returning to the instrument that will make your practice time more worthwhile. So remember little and often is better than a lot, less often.

Remember, little and often is best!

About The Keyboard

Although there are many different makes and types of electronic keyboard, they all follow a similar design with similar features. The instruction manual that comes with your keyboard will tell you a bit more about your particular instrument. Most keyboards will look like this and will include the common features listed below:

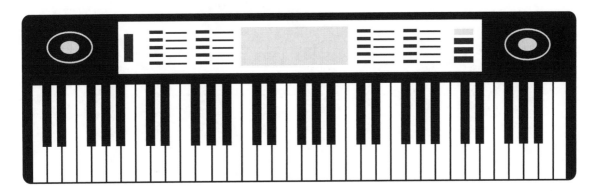

Can you find the following on your keyboard?

Two speakers — this is where the sound comes out!

The buttons — you will find two main sets of buttons on your keyboard. The position of these will be different depending on the make of your keyboard. Check your manual to find out which set of buttons on yours do the following:

Accompaniment/rhythm — these buttons allow you to choose a rhythm style when using accompaniments. Look for styles such as 'Disco' or 'Rock'.

Voice/tone/sounds — these select which melody sound the keyboard uses. Try a few out. Some will suit certain styles of music more than others.

Some keyboards also include **record** and **play** buttons too. These allow you to record your playing and play it back.

The Keyboard

The keyboard section of your instrument is based on the piano keyboard and is laid out in exactly the same way. Notice that the black notes are grouped in pairs and in threes:

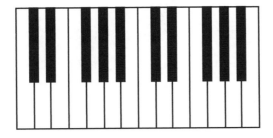

Playing Position

Always sit with your back straight on a suitable stool/chair. Your forearms should be at the same level as the keyboard. Your hands should never reach up to the keys.

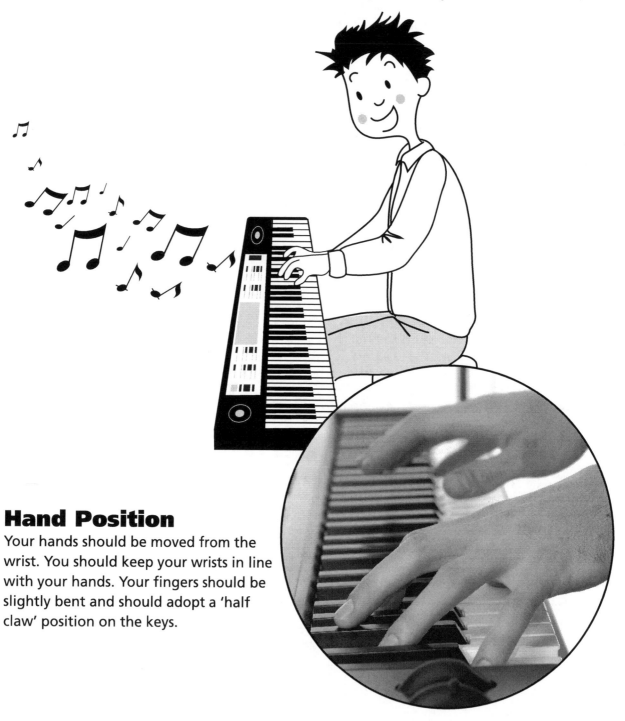

Hand Position

Your hands should be moved from the wrist. You should keep your wrists in line with your hands. Your fingers should be slightly bent and should adopt a 'half claw' position on the keys.

Your Fingers

The fingers of both your hands are numbered to help us know which fingers should play which notes. The thumb is number 1 on each hand:

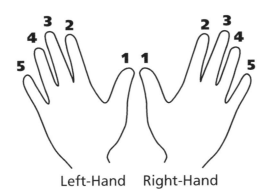

Left-Hand   Right-Hand

Middle C

The white note to the left of the pair of black notes on your keyboard is called '**C**'.
The **C** note closest to the middle of your keyboard is called '**Middle C**'.

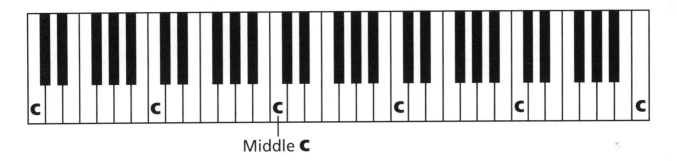

Middle **C**

Five Finger Playing Position

Eventually you will be using all your fingers of both hands to play your keyboard. To start with, let's just look at the right hand. As good discipline you should practice playing with your thumb on middle **C** and your other fingers each on a (subsequent) key of their own. So the right hand fingers would be as so: **finger 1** (thumb)– **C**, 2 – **D**, 3 – **E**, 4 – **F**, 5 – **G**.

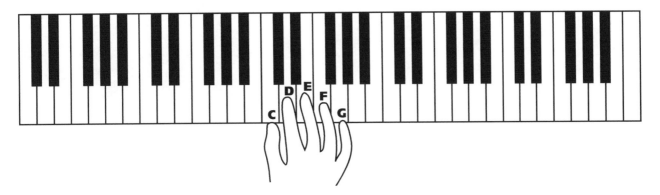

Knowing Your Notes

The notes on the music stave (see below) either sit in the spaces or on the lines. As notes go higher vertically on the stave they go higher in pitch. As they go lower vertically on the stave they go lower in pitch.

Octaves

Different keyboards have different numbers of keys. You will probably have between 4 and 5 Octaves of notes on your keyboard. An octave is 8 notes ('oct' meaning 8 like 'octopus' or 'octagon'). The same note up an octave sounds exactly the same but higher.

Ledger Lines

Music runs alphabetically from **A** to **G** and then starts again on **A**. When notes go above or below the stave we use ledger lines to keep track of how many spaces/lines down or up they are. So, the notes on your keyboard run like this:

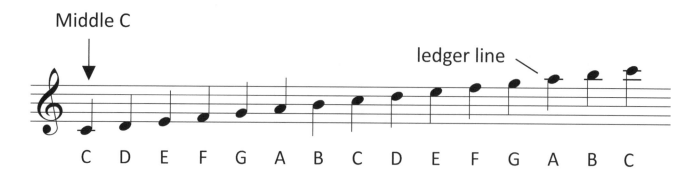

Other Musical Symbols

There are many symbols used in written music. Some are used to help us find our way around and some are used to give instructions along the way.

You will see the **Treble Clef** at the beginning of all keyboard music. This tells us where the notes are to be played. More advanced piano music has two staves. The top stave (or line of music) will always have a treble clef and will always show notes for your right hand.

The **Time Signature** is an important sign at the beginning of any piece of music. It tells us how many beats to count in each bar. At a beginners' level it is only really important to look at the top number. This will tell you how many beats there are in a bar.

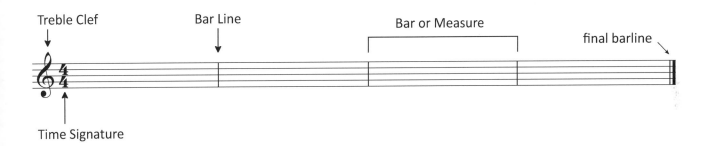

Notes and Note Lengths

Some notes last for longer than others. To show these different lengths notes look different according to their duration:

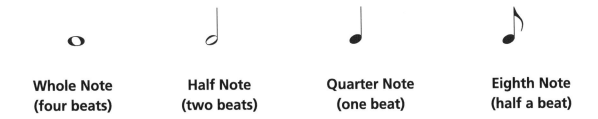

| **Whole Note** (four beats) | **Half Note** (two beats) | **Quarter Note** (one beat) | **Eighth Note** (half a beat) |

The Middle C

Let's start by playing the middle **C** note. To help you to read the notes at this early stage the note name will be written in the notehead of every note.

In the exercise below you will play **4** quarter notes in each bar. To help you stay in time, try counting to four as you play each note in the bar.

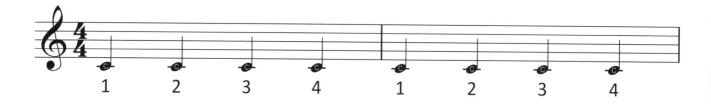

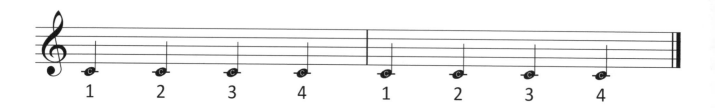

Let's try another two pieces with the middle **C** note. These will have words written below to help you with the rhythms. Try reading the words first before you try playing the **C** note along to the same rhythm. The main beats of the bar are written above the stave to remind you of the count.

Weekend Dreams

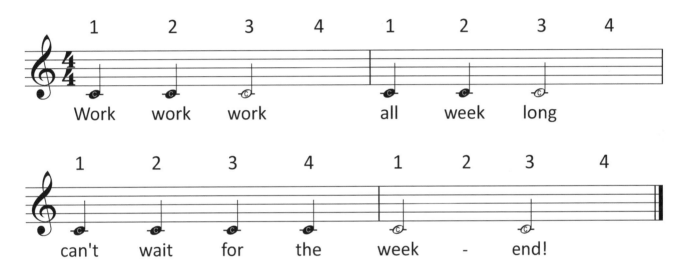

Playing Keyboard

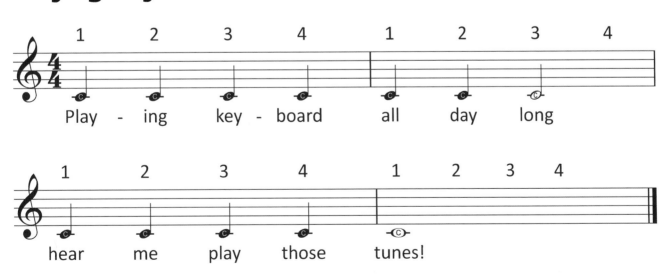

The Note D

Now try playing your **D** note using the exercise below. Remember to use finger number 2 of your right hand to play **D** and your thumb (finger 1) to play **C**.

The Note E

Your new note **E** is played with your 3rd finger. Try the following exercise using all three of your notes so far.

Quavers

So far we've only used whole notes, half notes and quarter notes. Our new note length is an eighth note. This is also known as a **quaver.** These last for half a beat. When counting eighth notes use **1 & 2 & 3 & 4 &**. This will help you with the rhythm.

Now we have 3 notes we can play a proper tune. Try changing your sound/tone to a flute or organ for this piece.

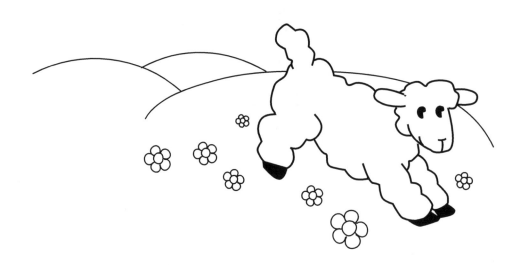

Mary Had A Little Lamb

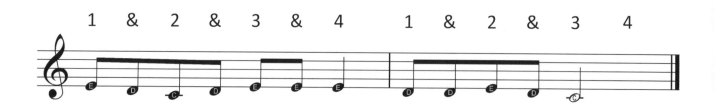

Repeat Marks

Sometimes you may want to play the same passage of music more than once. To save writing out that passage of music again we use repeat marks. When you see a closing repeat mark you either go back to the opening repeat mark or, if there isn't one, you go back to the beginning of the piece.

Try the piece below. Note when you get to the end you have an end repeat sign. This means you should go back to the beginning and play the whole piece again. Try a few different sounds/ tones for this piece.

Far From Home

3/4 or Waltz Time

So far all of our pieces and exercises have been written with 4 beats to a bar. **4/4** is probably the most common time signature you will come across. The other time signature you will see a lot is **3/4** (three beats in a bar). Commonly known as **Waltz time,** it was also a popular dance in the late 18th century.

Dotted Notes

A dot next to a note tells us to lengthen the note by half again. So a dotted half note (or 2 beat note) is worth 3 beats. This comes in very handy in waltz time!

Try playing '**Ballet Dance**' and remember to count 3 beats to each bar. Don't forget to play the dotted half note for 3 beats.

Ballet Dance

Other Time Signatures

You can also have two beats in a bar. This is written as **2/4** and is often called **March time**.

Try playing the piece below in **2/4**.

On The March

The Note F

Flat Bread And Beans

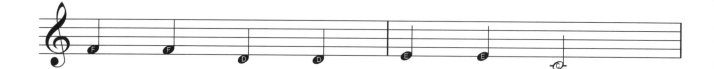

The Note G

The Long Ride Home

Single Finger Chords

So, you have an electronic keyboard and you've only used your right hand and the voices/tones section so far. Now it's time to see what your left hand can do!

Your keyboard will feature an accompaniment/auto chord section. Here you will be able to select a **rhythm** style (this will give you a drum beat) and a **single finger chord** option (sometimes known as 'auto accompaniment') for your **left hand**. Have a look at the instruction manual for your keyboard to see how this is shown on your instrument.

Most music you hear will be made up of a melody (or tune) AND a chord accompaniment. Chords are when you play more than 1 note at a time. **BUT** your keyboard allows you to select the lower keys (to the left of middle **C**) and use them to play chords with just one finger. Your keyboard will do the rest!

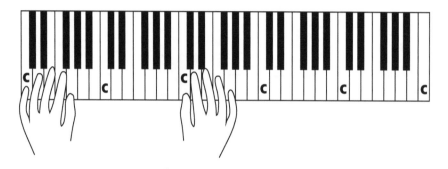

Here's how:

SELECT **THE SINGLE FINGER** CHORD FUNCTION

From now on you will see **chord names** written above the music in this book. The first single finger chord you will learn is **C**. Try holding down the lower **C** note as shown below. You'll hear the sound of more than one note. Even though you're only holding one down.

The C Single Finger Chord

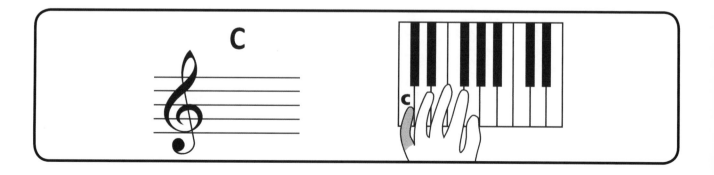

Rhythm/Style Auto Accompaniment

Now you're able to play chords with just one finger you can add an accompaniment/beat to get the sound of a whole band.

Turn on the **auto accompaniment** function

Select an accompaniment **style** or **rhythm**

A good style to start with is '**Rock**'. You usually find this near the top of the list of styles on your keyboard.

Select **sync start**

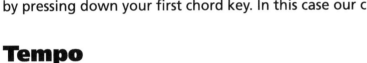

Having **Sync start** (or 'synchro start') on will allow you to start the song by pressing down your first chord key. In this case our chord key is **C**.

Tempo

The important thing as a beginner is to choose the right speed or tempo for your accompaniment. Look for up/down tempo buttons on your keyboard. These will allow you to change the speed of the backing.

Try 4 bars of accompaniment using your single finger **C** chord then press the **STOP** button. Count 4 beats to a bar to help you.

Now try holding down the chord with your left hand whilst playing this simple melody with your right hand:

The F Single Finger Chord

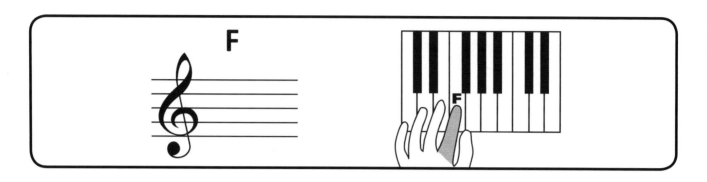

Most songs have more than one chord. Try the following exercise holding down your **C** chord for two bars then your **F** chord for two bars. Make sure **sync start** is on before you begin.

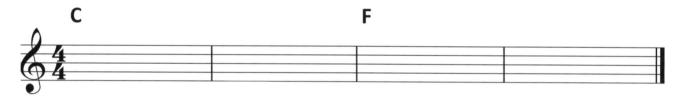

Now let's try a simple tune with changes between the **C** and **F** single finger chords. You might like to try another accompaniment style setting. How about '**Disco**' for this exercise?

The G Single Finger Chord

Now we have our third chord, **G**. Take the next piece slowly at first (remember to use your tempo buttons to change the accompaniment speed). Another fun rhythm style is '**Bossanova**'. Try it for this piece.

Treetop Blues

Ties

A **tie** joins two notes together— you only have to play the first note but it now lasts longer (its length **+** the length of the note it is tied to).

As well as ties, '**Oh When The Saints**' has an **anacrusis** or 'pick-up bar'. This is the 3-beat bar right at the beginning of the piece that acts as an introduction before the first main downbeat of your 'proper' bar 1. Also, notice the last bar only has 1 beat to make up for this irregular bar.

Don't start your accompaniment chord until you see your first **C** chord written above the music.

Try '**Brass**' as your sound/tone and '**Country**' as your rhythm style for this piece.

Oh When The Saints

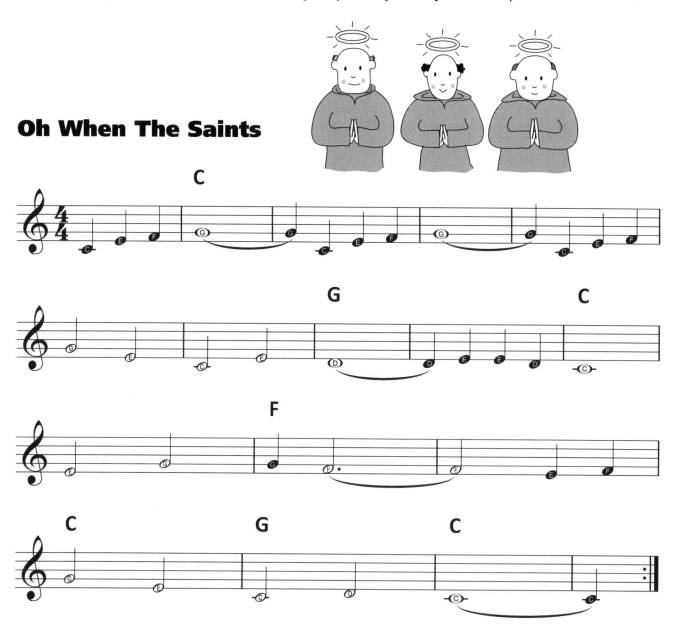

Rests

Rests tell us when not to play. Like notes, they last for different lengths of time. These different lengths are shown as different symbols:

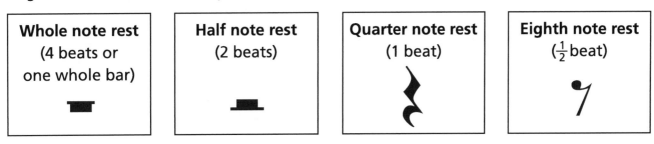

Whole note rest (4 beats or one whole bar)	Half note rest (2 beats)	Quarter note rest (1 beat)	Eighth note rest ($\frac{1}{2}$ beat)

Try playing the next piece with rests. Play it without the single finger chords first to get used to the rests in the melody.

Taking A Rest

Watch out for the opening repeat bar line in this piece. There is also a fast single finger chord change towards the end too! Don't forget to have fun experimenting with your sound/tone and rhythm style settings for each piece!

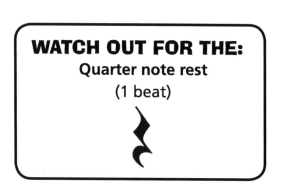

WATCH OUT FOR THE:
Quarter note rest
(1 beat)

The Grand Old Duke Of York

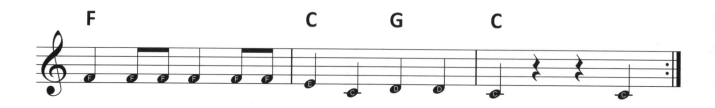

The Note A

To play your new note **A** you'll need to shift your right hand little finger (finger number 5) up to the next note. Watch out for it in **'Frere Jacques'** — the change from **G** to **A** is quite fast. It helps that this piece only has one chord! Use your thumb to play the **C** at the end of the run of eighth notes in the 3rd line then shift your fingers back to normal position for the last line.

Frere Jacques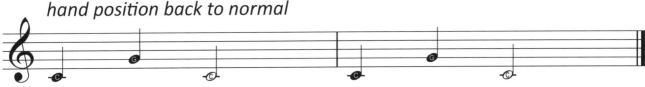

shift hand position

hand position back to normal

Time For Bed

The following two pieces have quite a lot going on so make sure you concentrate on your rhythms. They include ties and rests and also 'pushed' notes. This is when some of your notes are played just before the main beat — often as an eighth note tied to the next note. This is where music can get it's 'groove' from — it's ability to make you dance!

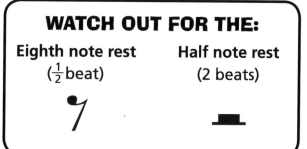

WATCH OUT FOR THE:

Eighth note rest ($\frac{1}{2}$ beat)

Half note rest (2 beats)

change hand position to play A

normal hand pos.

Drive Time

WATCH OUT FOR THE:

Whole note rest
(4 beats or
one whole bar)

Half note rest
(2 beats)

Quarter note rest
(1 beat)

Eighth note rest
($\frac{1}{2}$ beat)

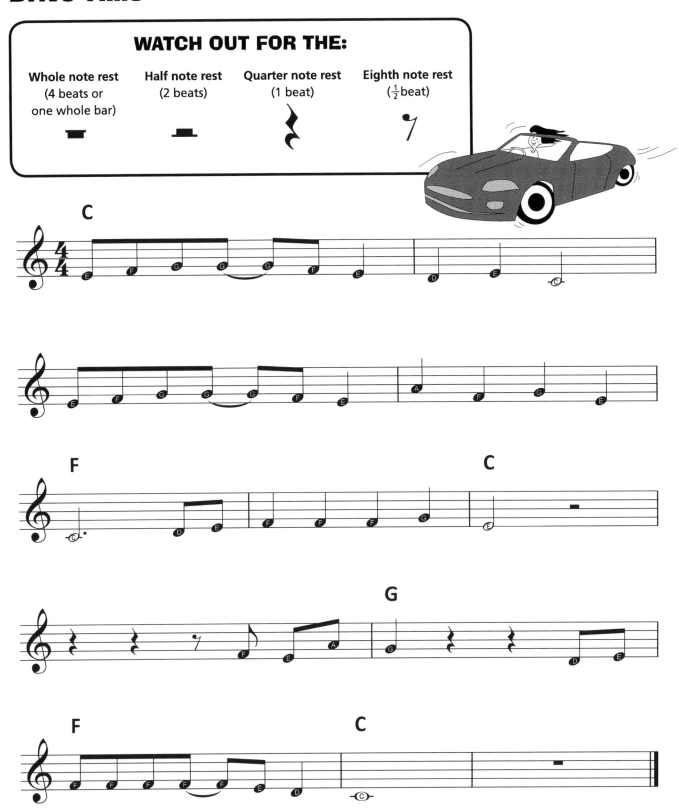

The Left Hand

Now it's time to start using your left hand to play single notes along with your right hand.

It's important you turn off your **'single finger chord'** and **'Sync Start'** function for this.

Your left hand should be positioned as follows:

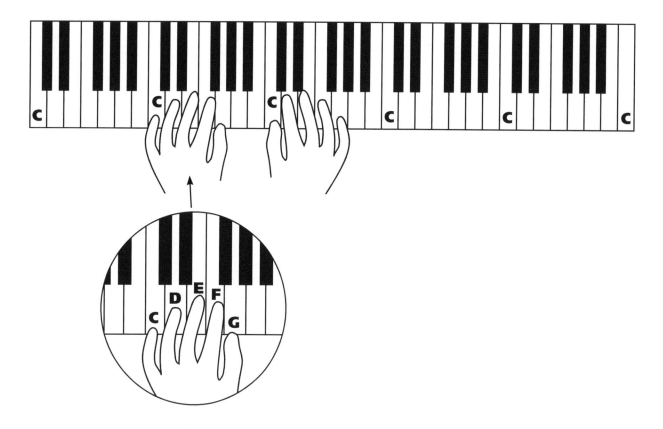

For notes in the left hand we use a separate stave with a different clef. This is called the **Bass clef**. Here are the left hand notes shown on the keyboard above, now written in the Bass clef below the Treble clef/right hand stave:

Bass Clef

Playing With Both Hands

Now let's try a very simple exercise to get you used to playing with both hands. Remember your fingering for your left hand notes. Make sure you start with your left hand little finger (finger 5) on the **C** below **middle C**.

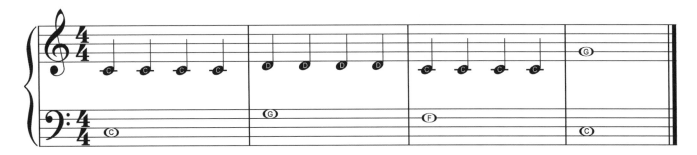

Now let's add some movement to your left hand part, keeping the right hand the same:

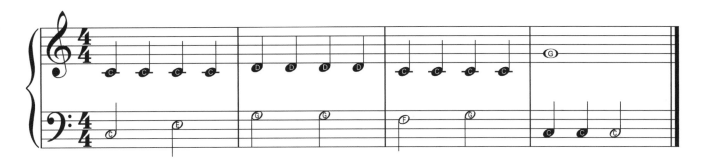

In this last exercise, both hands move around quite a bit. Take it really slowly to begin with then speed up gradually as your confidence increases.

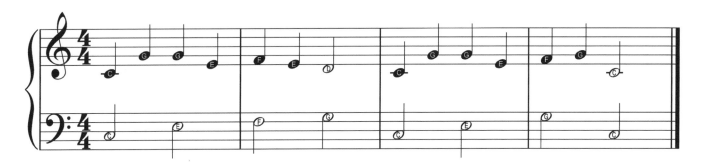

Now try playing the following two pieces. **Rolling Hills** gets your left hand moving whilst the right hand stays fairly simple.

Rolling Hills

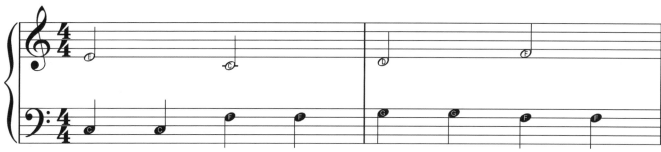

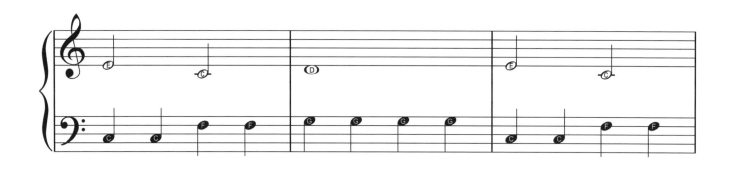

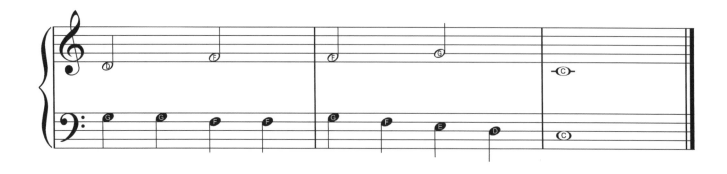

In **Sunrise** you'll find a busier right hand part with the left hand playing more of a supportive roll.

Sunrise

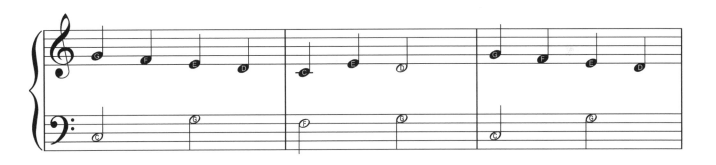

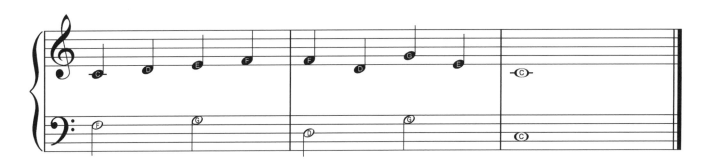

Oranges and Lemons

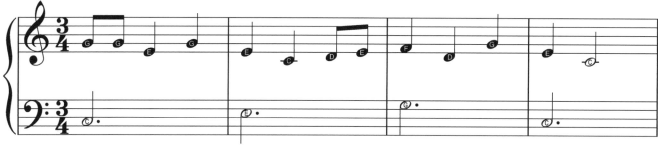

Playing The Melody With Both Hands

Oranges and Lemons and the exercises before it all use the left hand as accompaniment. In some pieces, however, the melody is shared between both hands. Have a look at '**Row, Row, Row Your Boat**' on the next page. Most of the melody is played in the left hand until the 4th line where the right hand steps in to play the **middle C**.

Row, Row, Row Your Boat

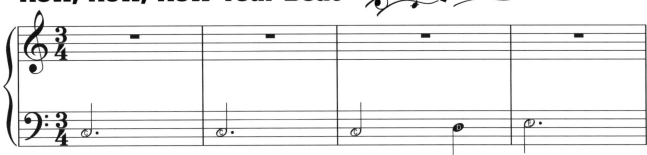

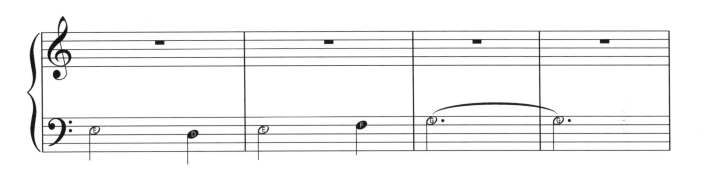

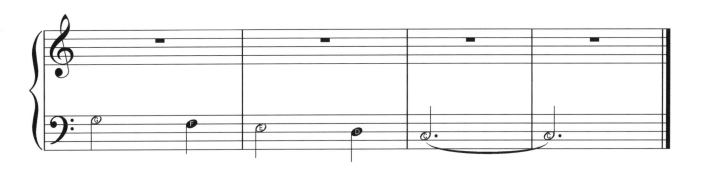

Slow Dance

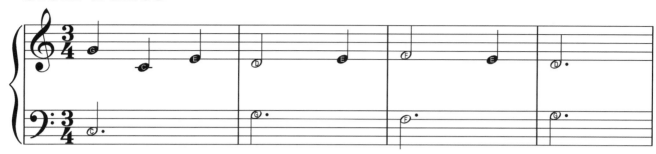

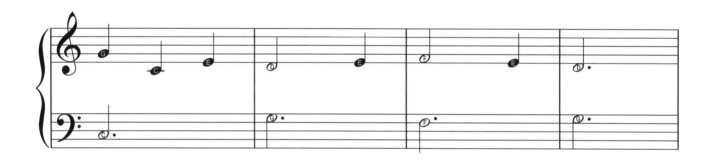

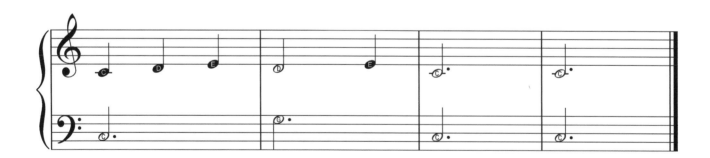

Jingle Bells

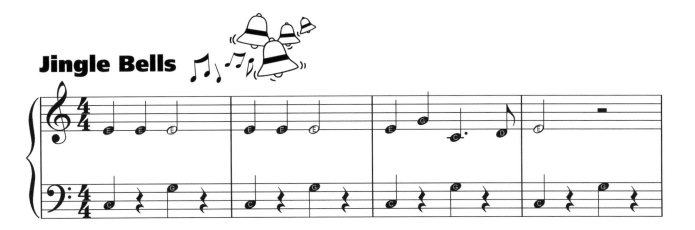

Playing Chords **C**, **F** & **G** With Both Hands

In most pop music today the keyboards are often used as an accompanying chordal instrument where the player will use both hands to play the chord progression or 'pattern' of the song. To illustrate this, we'll be using *fingerings* to help map out the position of your fingers.

Unlike the more 'classical' approach where the right hand plays the melody and always has a defined position, this pop style requires frequent position changes of the right hand. Let's start by looking at the hand positions for your three main chords, **C**, **F** and **G**.

The hand position for your **C** chord shown below shows a move away from the traditional '1 finger per key' positioning. Your second finger now stretches along to play the **E** note, whilst your 4th finger moves up to the **G**.

Chord **C**

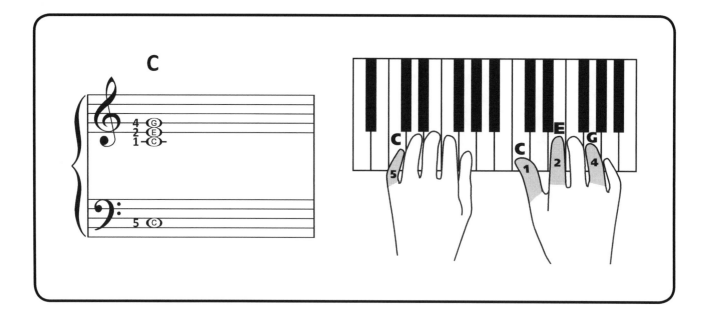

Chord F

In your **F** chord, your thumb remains on **C**, your 3rd finger plays the **F** note whilst your 5th finger plays the **A**. This is to help you move smoothly from the **C** chord. Your left hand uses finger 2 to play the **F** bass note.

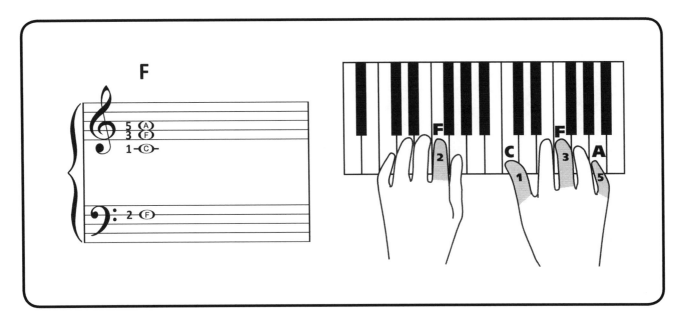

Chord G

And finally for your **G** chord your thumb now moves down to play the **B** note below **middle C**, your 2nd finger plays the **D** note whilst your 5th finger plays the **G**.

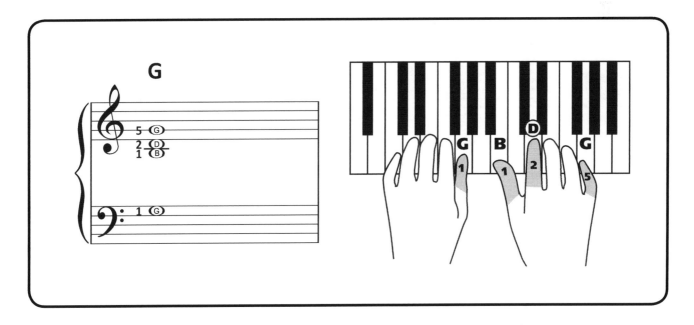

Let's Play Chords!

You may recognize the sound of these three chords when played together. They make up the **'three chord trick'** made infamous by blues and rock n roll. Play them slowly to start with then try a bit more movement as you go:

Exercise 1

Exercise 2

12 Bar Blues

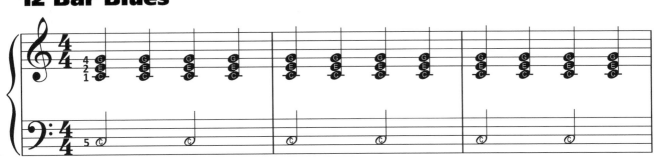

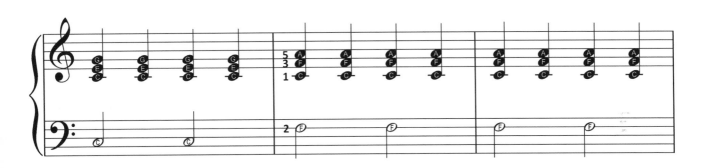

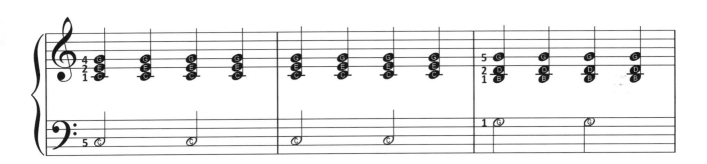

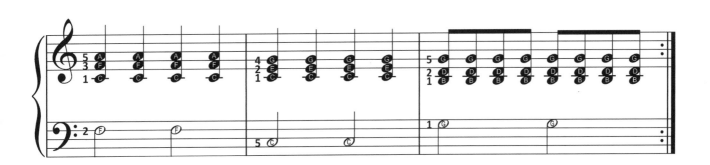

Quiz!

NAME THAT NOTE!

How many beats do each of these notes last for?

HALF/ONE/TWO/FOUR

HALF/ONE/TWO/FOUR

HALF/ONE/TWO/FOUR

HALF/ONE/TWO/FOUR

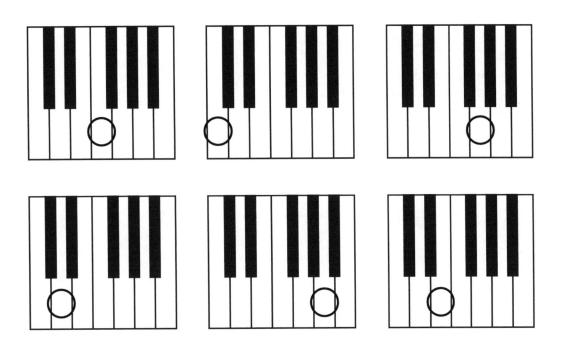

Can you fill in the correct RIGHT HAND NOTE names on the keys above?

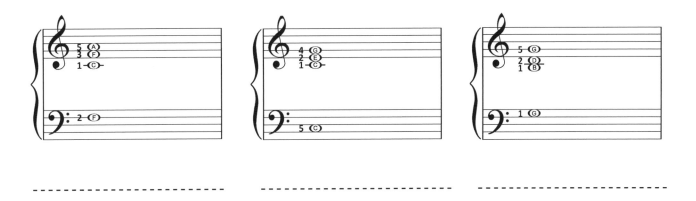

- -

Can you name the CHORDS above?

Right Hand Notes

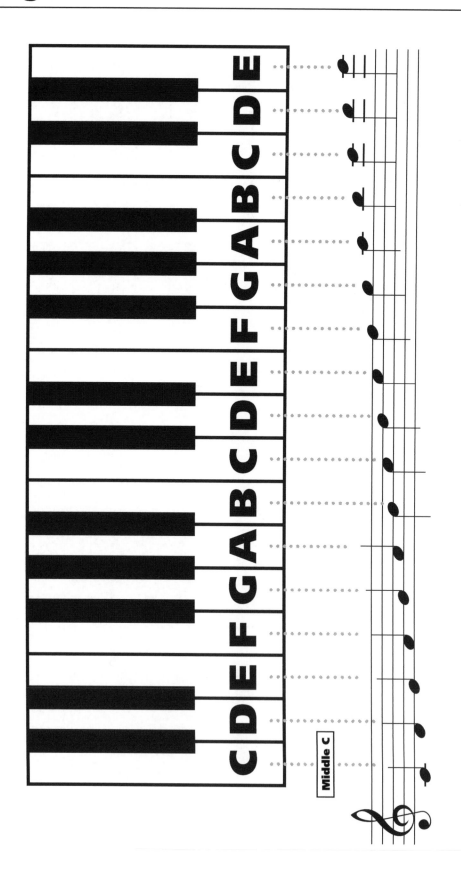

Left Hand Notes

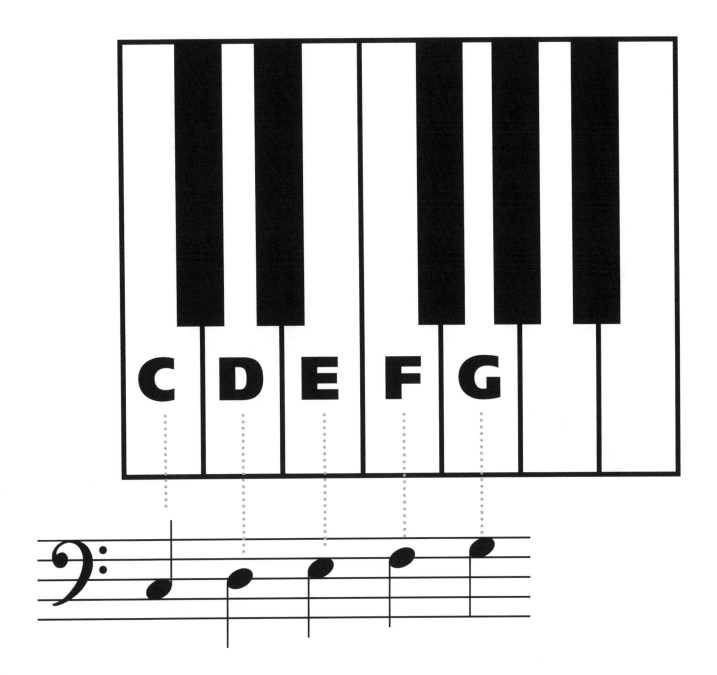

Chords With Both Hands

C

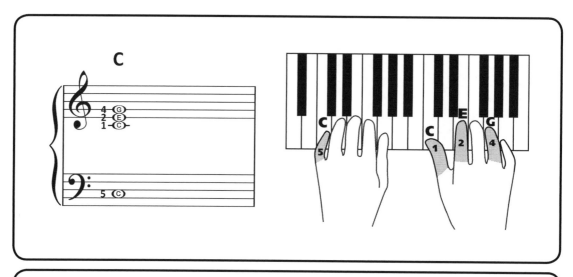

F

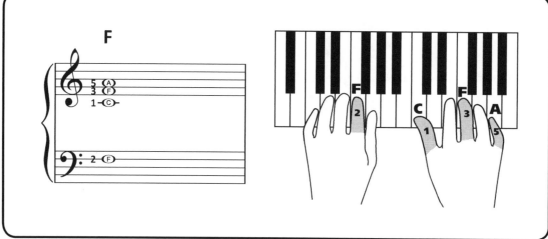

G

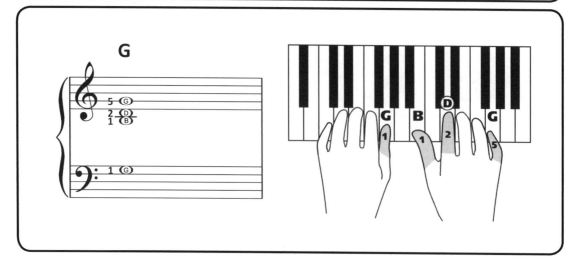

Cut out the letters below and stick them to the correct keys on your keyboard!

NOTES:

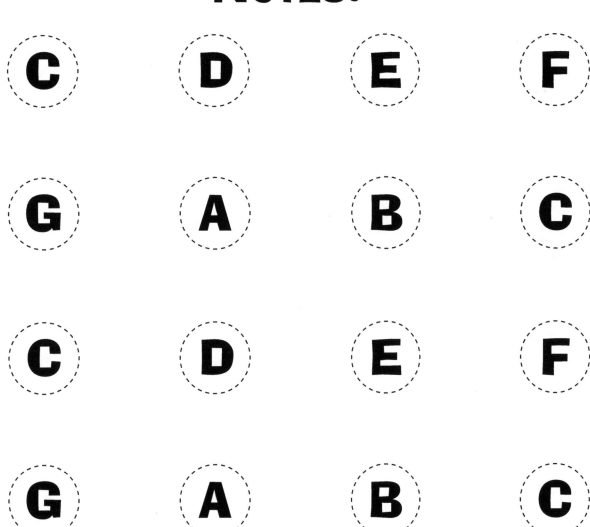

MORE GREAT MUSIC BOOKS FROM KYLE CRAIG!

 **How To Play UKULELE —** A Complete Guide for Absolute Beginners

978-1-908-707-08-6

 **My First UKULELE —** Learn to Play: Kids

978-1-908-707-11-6

 **Easy UKULELE Tunes**

978-1-908707-37-6

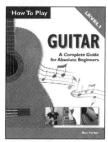 **How To Play GUITAR —** A Complete Guide for Absolute Beginners

978-1-908-707-09-3

 **My First GUITAR —** Learn to Play: Kids

978-1-908-707-13-0

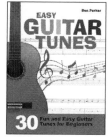 **Easy GUITAR Tunes**

978-1-908707-34-5

 **How To Play KEYBOARD —** A Complete Guide for Absolute Beginners

978-1-908-707-14-7

 **My First KEYBOARD —** Learn to Play: Kids

978-1-908-707-15-4

 **Easy KEYBOARD Tunes**

978-1-908707-35-2

 **How To Play PIANO —** A Complete Guide for Absolute Beginners

978-1-908-707-16-1

 **My First PIANO —** Learn to Play: Kids

978-1-908-707-17-8

 **Easy PIANO Tunes**

978-1-908707-33-8

 **How To Play HARMONICA —** A Complete Guide for Absolute Beginners

978-1-908-707-28-4

 **My First RECORDER —** Learn to Play: Kids

978-1-908-707-18-5

 **Easy RECORDER Tunes**

978-1-908707-36-9

 **How To Play BANJO —** A Complete Guide for Absolute Beginners

978-1-908-707-19-2

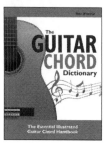 **The GUITAR Chord Dictionary**

978-1-908707-39-0

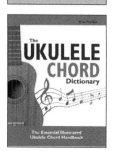 **The UKULELE Chord Dictionary**

978-1-908707-38-3

Manufactured by Amazon.ca
Bolton, ON

13295187R00028